Transitional Spaces

Kate Behrens was born in 1959. Two Rivers Press published *The Beholder* (2012), *Man with Bombe Alaska* (2016) and *Penumbra* (2019). She lives in Oxfordshire and has one child.

By the same author

Kate Behrens, *The Beholder* (Two Rivers Press, 2012)
Kate Behrens, *Man with Bombe Alaska* (Two Rivers Press, 2016)
Kate Behrens, *Penumbra* (Two Rivers Press, 2019)

Also by Two Rivers Poets

David Attwooll, *The Sound Ladder* (2015)
William Bedford, *The Dancers of Colbek* (2020)
Adrian Blamires & Peter Robinson (eds.), *The Arts of Peace* (2014)
Charles Baudelaire, *Paris Scenes* translated by Ian Brinton (2021)
Conor Carville, *English Martyrs* (2019)
David Cooke, *A Murmuration* (2015)
David Cooke, *Sicilian Elephants* (2021)
Terry Cree, *Fruit* (2014)
Claire Dyer, *Eleven Rooms* (2013)
Claire Dyer, *Interference Effects* (2016)
Claire Dyer, *Yield* (2021)
John Froy, *Sandpaper & Seahorses* (2018)
James Harpur, *The Examined Life* (2021)
A. F. Harrold, *The Point of Inconvenience* (2013)
Maria Teresa Horta, *Point of Honour* translated by Lesley Saunders (2019)
Ian House, *Nothing's Lost* (2014)
Ian House, *Just a Moment* (2020)
Gill Learner, *Chill Factor* (2016)
Gill Learner, *Change* (2021)
Sue Leigh, *Chosen Hill* (2018)
Sue Leigh, *Her Orchards* (2021)
Becci Louise, *Octopus Medicine* (2017)
Mairi MacInnes, *Amazing Memories of Childhood, etc.* (2016)
Steven Matthews, *On Magnetism* (2017)
Henri Michaux, *Storms under the Skin* translated by Jane Draycott (2017)
René Noyau, *Earth on Fire and other Poems* translated by Gérard Noyau
    with Peter Pegnall (2021)
James Peake, *Reaction Time of Glass* (2019)
James Peake, *The Star in the Branches* (2022)
Tom Phillips, *Recreation Ground* (2012)
John Pilling & Peter Robinson (eds.), *The Rilke of Ruth Speirs:
    New Poems, Duino Elegies, Sonnets to Orpheus & Others* (2015)
Peter Robinson, *Foreigners, Drunks and Babies: Eleven Stories* (2013)
Peter Robinson, *The Constitutionals: A Fiction* (2019)
Peter Robinson & David Inshaw, *Bonjour Mr Inshaw* (2020)

Lesley Saunders, *Cloud Camera* (2012)
Lesley Saunders, *Nominy-Dominy* (2018)
Lesley Saunders, *This Thing of Blood & Love* (2022)
Jack Thacker, *Handling* (2018)
Susan Utting, *Fair's Fair* (2012)
Susan Utting, *Half the Human Race* (2017)
Jean Watkins, *Scrimshaw* (2013)
Jean Watkins, *Precarious Lives* (2018)

Transitional Spaces

Kate Behrens

First published in the UK in 2022 by Two Rivers Press
7 Denmark Road, Reading RG1 5PA.
www.tworiverspress.com

© Kate Behrens 2022

The right of the poet to be identified as the author of this work
has been asserted by her in accordance with the Copyright, Designs
and Patents Act of 1988.

All rights reserved. No part of this publication may be reproduced,
stored in or introduced into a retrieval system, or transmitted,
in any form, or by any means (electronic, mechanical, photocopying,
recording or otherwise) without the prior written permission
of the publisher.

ISBN 978-1-909747-94-4

1 2 3 4 5 6 7 8 9

Two Rivers Press is represented in the UK by Inpress Ltd
and distributed by Ingram Publisher Services UK.

Cover design and illustration by Sally Castle
Text design by Nadja Guggi and typeset in Janson and Parisine

Printed and bound in Great Britain by Severn, Gloucester

Acknowledgements

Some of these poems, or earlier versions of them, first appeared in *Wild Court*, May 2019, *Noon* #16, *The High Window*, issue 16, *Stand* 18.2, *Poetry Salzburg Review*, no 38, the Australian journal *Axon: Creative Endeavours*, issue 10.1 and in translation in the Macedonian *Rast*, issue 21–22; many thanks to their editors.

I am indebted to Claire Dyer for her help with structuring the book, to Simon Frazer for his invaluable overview and to Ian House for the acuity of comments on some of the poems. Thanks to my family for their loving support of this collection.

Contents

I.

Inside the Poem | 2
Dream of a Motherless Child | 3
Waking Reflection | 4
Your Sister's Tapestry Cushion | 5
Ingenuity | 6
One Moment | 7
Neck Traction | 8
The Carpenter's Daughter's Long Engagement | 9
Foreign Childhood | 10
Reworking | 11
Pushing through Sultry Days | 12
Vehicle | 13
Flashing Up | 14

II.

The Naked Seventies | 16
Colours of Paris, 1984 | 19
Compensation | 21
The Tree Surgeon | 22
Mad Messages | 23
Dream Lover | 24
Too Late | 25
Hints from Colour | 26
Chalkland | 28
Narcissi on Valentine's Day | 29

III.

Weightlessness | 32
Punctuation | 33
The Look of Transition | 34
First Steps | 36
Dreams of Our Missing | 37

Anniversary Poem | 38
Respite | 39
Deep Winter | 40

IV.

Unattended Baggage | 42
Wanted | 43
Shoppers in Mayfair | 45
The Hidden Flaw | 46
Tate Modern Pigeon | 47
Early Days – Half-Dreaming Your Bike Route Home | 48
For a Better World | 49
Oxford Users and their Dogs | 50
Construction | 51
Veils Failing | 52
Something in the Air, March 2020 | 54
UK, Autumn 2020 | 55
A Perfect Storm, Christmas Eve | 56

V.

Elective Surgery | 60
Lacuna | 62
Communication | 63
Mind in the Garden | 64
Incy Wincy Spider | 65
Breakdown | 66
Muntjac | 67
Two Poets | 68
Untitled | 70
Ghazal for Us All | 71
Nothing Changes | 72

Notes | 74

For Nicky Loutit
and, as always, for Jack

I.

Inside the Poem

You open the door, proceed down a line,
look out where a window juts,
at white sky over a 'scape
of changeable signs –
return.

The next time there's no delay
returning, a playful swerve or diversion
swings you
toward an anteroom, and so it goes on;
en route there are steps up
or down,

things displayed or under the ground, the sense
always of more to come, the line's
hook (see, it has many dimensions)
that mustn't drag you, but gently tug

not at the body or mind, but both – for something
you'd been deaf and blind to, knew.

Dream of a Motherless Child

Remember the pin point
zeroed in on
             (surreal sharpness)
creeping along the rim of the sea

....

It never pierces a white sea-skin

Along that horizon
   held down
   fused to it
   emptied of air
   slowed   dumbed down
   wait for cataclysm to come

The world exploding and a sudden
vertiginous rising up
of all human horizons
makes pin-less rimless
                     un-witnessed

this forever upside-

            down-ness
with vague shrouded objects'

unquantifiable distances
tangled in black

Tangled in black
   the no-breath

               The no   breath

Waking Reflection

They bob and merge: leaf shadows.
Wind-bullied trees gather
and sink. In distant fields
sheets of plastic sail
against the estuary's eyeball white.

Against the estuary's sky-
white, sheets of plastic sail
and sink in distant fields.
Wind-bullied trees gather.

It bobs, is submerged: our shadow
(there is too much light).
When will we know we're
still asleep?

Your Sister's Tapestry Cushion

i.m my grandmother, 'Culler' and her sister, Den

In this view
weft-faced yews (Uccello darks)
strew the escarpment's
mint, grey-green, plaster, white.

Her mind was stitched
in yours, yours into mine
(those colours spoke like a mother tongue).

From a distance, it's leaping wildness,
the in-out of things
sewn up. Shadow and lightness.

We would sit on your sofa in drifts
of Silk Cut smoke, Ma Griffe.
Tonal shifts made patterns

to lean on, with the thick curtains
drawn on blue cedars.

Ingenuity

The child made a hut out of barbed wire,
huddled inside. All around

fairies glittered, some disguised
as dandelion clocks,
others, glimpsed through Brutalist arches,
as dust motes. Their gift
was immortality.

Over and over disaster hit:
Tramping Man, their flooded lilies.
One got pneumonia
but they had the injection to save her.
When their tree got struck by lightning,
all escaped.

The child flung notes to her mum
out of the window

into the London street:
night fairies sped them to Heaven.

One Moment

What if that tenderness
context leant us for nature
became the vanity of humans,
so nature – inalienable,
alien –
no longer means
more than one atom,
one universe?

Neck Traction

Primroses, moss-promises,
fairyland complexity;
she can't quite see it.

The flower basket smacks
of Gran's handle on things in emergencies.

Roomscape's white, or the boy
who pees in a bottle (that's not a bottle).

Mums. *The duck ornament's not in her palm.*

Whiteness gets blurred
as lines of wet
steepen the temples

reach acres of duckless sheet,
but she keeps out
long-coming waves with a thinking chest.

In a hurting coolness, through all
lopsidedness

Gran might come back
in that dress like reflections in the Thames,

walk her out
through box aromas.

The Carpenter's Daughter's Long Engagement

I loved Guido's hideous cupboard,
its stiff façade
(a little neo-fascist

but so accidentally),
how unflinchingly
it stood by her, prepared

with anticipatory gleams
and squeaks from double sheets
she'd one day be ravished in.

Her road shot like a snake
out from foundations of lace,
miles from meltdown or earthquake

then weaved like a dot-to-dot:
motorino-to-Fiat, Fiat-to-Sienese-flat
oh, to-*perbenismo*

but we were just fourteen,
shuddered on that line
between disgust and longing.

My road resembled her mum's
fettuccine, but I was almost
Lucia in her house.

Foreign Childhood

Did this *belong* to him once?
The place assaults with kisses.
To reject its embrace isn't a choice.
The faint hills recede, paper-thin disguise
of a paradise first stolen, then lost. Forsaken –
alive still inside him: like forbidden love re-awoken.

Reworking

There is a dog and a pig,
they belong to her dad who is drunk.
Why do you feed the dog each day, the pig every other?

He looks like a shuttered
window. Words skim off him.
The pig, so bald, blunders
from hunger at the edges of dream.

She searches for words her dad would like
to make him see the urgency,
politely. *And it must be the right
kind of food, potatoes*

*kill pigs, and each bit
must be sliced?*
He loads up the dog's dish,
keeps the pig at bay with his foot

and the dog wags its furry brownness
while the pig watches.
She stutters through different words,
forces them into

incontrovertible groupings
and the pig watches.
Her words fall off the wall
of his face, the pig starves;

hour after hour, in real time
that dog's dish is filled,
the dog wags its tail,
the dream nails its message in.

Pushing through Sultry Days

…because the gorse seeds crack, and dappled ground
is sand (though here there is no tang of pine)…

because that sound of buzzing flies surrounds
the thickened silence of the dead

combined with faeces' summer reek, and now the click of bulrushes
evokes malefic beings that darted through a lost *maquis*

and dart on still, through these Black Poplars' shivered susurrus.

Vehicle

Love renews with each purred breath
(it sleeps on my roof):
no conditions,
no solutions.

Distillation
of all such inhuman
provocation.

Plus stillness:
the slow stars stilled
its tongue.

Flashing Up

After a short film, *Nour (Reflection)*, by Akram Zaatari

It seems you too were a motherless child
but I miss the beginning.
It's your wide-eyed bargaining
with magic feels familiar
in this room you flicker over:

child, smeared mirror held up
to bounce around
the smut and squeeze of days
in Saida's worn passageways,

to inch along long walls,
follow each blaze
(your small reflected gaze, a smile
slowed by epiphany).

In unlaced huge shoes,
between their businesses
and such recent babyhood,
you flash up naked truths

as lies; all we see
is pools of light.

II.

The Naked Seventies

I.

The emptiness keeps driving –
means something like you've done him
wrong. But you guess you'll do it again.

Perhaps you were too young,
perhaps he regrets that the fling
with your mum was only a fling.

Dark arches balloon night's unstable words,
pointers flick like deep-sea fishes.
His hand on the gear stick
is like a lost caress.

II.

Lucas's moles: inversed constellations.
He says, 'I'm playing the waiting game.'
Neither of you know what it means.

You sleep in the blue room
curtained by indecision.
Instead of the moon, it's orange streetlight
makes you insignificant.

Longing to love him is almost sufficient,
but the city imposes
a map on each of your histories,

the lost and the exes
in differing blues, then dawn unravels
a confusion of London planes,
casts shadow

on what has happened,
what has not.

III.

Rett shoots through the lanes, headlights off, to check
for oncoming cars at bends.

After sex, he lies in bed counting
old girlfriends; he likes them
anorexic, snow stuffed up vaginas.
He doesn't care enough
to notice your laughter is false.
He likes to slaughter animals
but you'd forgotten or never knew,
till his obituary spills it thirty-five years on.

IV.

In-love, you were almost re-birthed
since you were also dreamt,
each as the lost part of a whole,
each, flawless individual.
I love you, you said, I love you,
you a wound men dove into
before they found there broken glass,
before the carcasses of love
turned explosive and transparent.

VI.

The best remained in the silence of dreamers,
included belief
in a body's truthfulness
which made a kiss
a portent, sex, into a high art
(that couldn't be mastered
by the whole world, surely?) –

a yes that stoppered breath,
a troubled yes, but still a yes
on mirrored lips
breeding wild sweetness, wildfire.

Colours of Paris, 1984

Pearl:
Luxembourg gardens. Gilles and I break in. Orange trees
 on wheels,
trundled from night's *orangerie*, take up position – and the pink
 curtain lifts.

Payne's Grey:
After the launderette, the cinema club is screening all day
 Hitchcock in a season of picturesque rain, fat cloud on slate.

Vandyke Brown:
I'm painting Nena's cabinet, but she says the *faux marbre* is not
 triste enough; I
copy the sparrow-hues of her flat, the *je ne sais quoi* in her *désespoir*.

Tabby:
Benoît of *deux chats* and *deux petites amies*, sings at the Opéra
 as Glue and Fenouille hurl themselves off his furniture.

Emerald:
Belleville, and the May Day Roma sell *muguets*.

Purple:
Heaped lilac branches around a church; our stolen armfuls, dripping.

Umber:
Oeufs en gelée.

Phthalo Blue:
Waiting for the film job to happen.

Transparency:
Hookers on our street, the yelling *vitrier* with his barrow of glass.

When did it all end, where did we belong? Our youthful hearts:
 not padlocked to bridges but cast adrift on an onrush of moments.

I stumbled into bed with Paris:
not a love-affair, so much
as the unfamiliar seeming
more familiar than home.
City of rounded corners
and that muted palette,
it wore the look of quieter stories:
no *demains*, no *hiers*.

Compensation

The unsaid, the unsayable,
duty paid
freight this enormous parcel.
It arrives, an unexploded
sadness.

He would prefer
a dandelion, given
from a moment's love,
will not take on

a present beribboned in guilt
though it tickles his heart.
Her not-being-there...
God. It hurts.

He will strip it of all
accoutrements, give it
to someone who can
tell it straight.

The Tree Surgeon

He stands as if in 'twisted perspective'
between your irises and spurge,
head faced forward.
Stilled.

She thinks of the counter language
of trees, this musculature harnessed
to a series of lethal acts.

Raising his arms,
he wields the right-angled shaft, tenderly
shaves off bright new growth,

inches onwards, knowing
without looking down, where plants are,
unaware that time passes.

He peels off the silver top.
The frieze of hedge on which he's iconographic
darkens. Box leaves

spill onto parched earth, point-up the nascent
(unbelievable, when she looks back on it:
desire, unchanged.
Invincible as wild Violas).

Mad Messages

Cryptic, unconnected
as bits of storm

wreckage blown in
from afar

two texts roll in,
apropos of nothing!

They're clinging
to patterns of floating

words broken off
the mainland.

All three of you have changed.
You can't afford

their proffered minds.
It's taken a while

to swim here.

Dream Lover

Next to a Spanish river, I tell him
my body is ruined.
Not existing, he doesn't mind:
I like your differences.

With metallic water,
time unravels blue streets,
silver mohicans – they're palm trees –
behind them, tall town houses
of the belonging children.

Be careful what you wish for, I say,
unwrapping two *bocadillos,*
tapping at tunes enveloped in dream.

The moon picks out flat stones,
brings us to great longing
we are ill-prepared for

since we near the death of all
we had once believed in,
as I kiss cruel air.

Too Late

She paces about the hills and earth cracks.
Her front teeth ache where rabbits failed
to scrape a living. Air
has upended routine, is emptied.
Bluer.

She sees him: youth disguised
as an old man.
He fights the diurnal flicker
with his new weightlessness
and implodes at the edges of vision –

she tells him she always loved him.
He hoots, now a ruffled owl
awoken by the closeness
of dying:
it's you who's in denial here.

That familiar pattern of holes:
the near-meeting tips of garlic mustard
leaves lacing the hedgerow.

Hints from Colour

I. Off-White

There was no way, we knew,
in the build-up

(fields hispid with lit shoots,
may blossom, unwieldy.
Like sodden bridal veils).

There was no danger, we knew,
carefully picking words
that said this is not to do with *all that*.

II. French Blues

Through my ceiling
your navy throat rumbles
with *ronronnements*,
stops. (Are you dreaming?)

Between ceruleans
and human unease –
immediate sleep.

You roost there, fearless
as stars.

Snore me another pigeon-berceuse
(for *le cafard*).

III. Glow-worm Green

like a long-ago Christmas
Pifco-lit ...

These are insular girls.
Not shakers. Or movers.

They starved for this, the night of a lifetime.
Blue moonlit clouds, blue whitebeam trees
clash with their precision.

'Fuck me to death,' green murmurs …
so each luciferous abdomen snuffs it.
A hundred *petites morts* turned grand.

The hillside's strewn
with darknesses.

Chalkland

How to disintegrate: in the faecal-honey smells
from a lit field of rape
after a *coup-de-foudre* reveals
you are, after all, see-through
and swallows are swallowed by eaves
in the derelict farm

(transitional spaces
where only skies mark
where inner-to-outer sheltered,
and the white-stomached mouse).

Narcissi on Valentine's Day

The body's long-ingested springs
spring in the veins,

though quietened
re-spark darkened blood,

as trumpets of lighter red lift
and suggest

the lilt and tilt of a loved one's mouth
shifting in dream.

III.

Weightlessness

To the memory of my father

In the Bar Calypso your face reappears,
though that was razed
so soon after they seemed
to say 'an era is over'
and coloured high-rises, a gentler emptiness
tower where your bundle of bones
no longer floats down the mattress.

Walls bear pictures of ours
as those you admired
and dowager seagulls belt out that cadence they always
descended, but the balcony's rusted,
leafier now there is time

to spend. I am a tourist in bright bits
that can now hold us
(untrammelled by adjectives, see, we are
weightless), remember

the load of these feet in your murkiest corners,
as a slightness still leaps
from your wheelchair on cobbles
or you catch me out
with the one short-sighted eye
on the edges of Calle de las Huertas …

and yes, when we stir you
into the earth at Celas, Dad
(over your dog, as you desired),
the ashes slink off like wildness returning.
Your praying mantis prays.

Punctuation

Tortoiseshells, trapped
between huge sash windows,
were slowing like last
hours, or a string of prayers
flapped in the Himalayas

and they can't have been him
when that Comma flitted
'only thirty minutes later',
to settle on her – a windward

Komma: 'piece cut off'
or a pause's
small insistence, *forwards*,
fluttered?

She and a Comma
whisper, no:
these are your ideas.

The Look of Transition

I.

This dun unrolling doesn't reflect us.
Seagulls rest secretive
eyes under hollow bones.
A cut-out boat is tissue-thin,
horizon's a bent
cane.

It waits to ping now
into then.

II.

Night's waves shelve silvers for blacks,
individuate

in rhythms not ours,
and ours.

Alien heartbeats the hours
uncover

in failing bodies
(now flashed with graces
darks allow)

stop.

Each wave sheds silvers
for blacks,

retreats.

III.

The pendulum's swung:
rooks flung over
the pine, back again,

pattern a raucous conversation,
leave a ghost-looping
where questions
stuck.

First Steps

There is a nothing
anoints him (like the sun shines on)
after the worst has happened –

nothing
cluttered on numbness.
But it's really a thing

unfolding, like clots,
inflammation, proliferation …
Tissue remodelling.

     *

Now conversation,
insolent skies that persist
in blinking,

are not enemies, but intimacies
re-becoming his.

Dreams of Our Missing

Where are loved ones who never feature?
You are mostly hanging around
all but a life-long longing,
offer a weekend then disappear,

leave the glittering sea
like a trick where absence gets handed over
to light – as if that might help
for more than a minute, given it all!

As your own flicks its trail
of promise and wake of litter
into the day, then another dream.

What material is it you live in?
Not oxygen. Not even
remembrance.

Animate, yet essences …?
Run amok with last words.

Anniversary Poem

i.m of my twin, Sophie Behrens

The thrown-sand sound of rain,
slurred dictator, memory,
needling dark.

Pure feeling was the first born.

As a face appears
clearer than it has,
from imminent proximity

the afterlife of love
wakes us survivors,

yet each unclear breath
struggles out from buried love.

Hills never listened
to human solutions.

Precision around abstraction –
flowers outlive each night.

Respite

The starling, the starling and stars
startling and sequence of burst
silences: dread stunned dormant

for now. How delicate the reached-out-to,
delivered through flesh, and the cut
of hope on a walkway. You'd forgotten
you weren't ancient.

Deep Winter

'Non sono mai stato
tanto
attacato alla vita.'
— Giuseppe Ungaretti

The trees shed a strange ice
like colourless kaleidoscope
glass. The air
is heavy, at last
unclenched but inclined
towards ground
like someone in shock at a death.
What remains, challenges,
from so high above us
is an unreadable language:
untellable stories
locked into brightness,
white traceries
on beech and birch,
larch and a silver fir –
the thought returns:
we're fortunate
to be here.

IV.

Unattended Baggage

I.

Halitosis, sandwiches… two clashed languages fight it out,
  one in each ear-hole.
Raindrops (close-by worlds, refracted) startle as the bus brakes
  – wobble a peacock's fanned tail in poppling lines across the
  windscreen

II.

She texts on her mobile but there's no signal (we're below ground). *Ping,
  ping.* Ping.
Eyes, stumbled-on slits pinioning mine, hex as she pings out
  'ammunition'. Pings tattoo it: untellable rage.

III.

Crawling, blind-reversing into a young woman's Nikes across the
aisle, he bobs under other seats, resurfaces for air, hair's a phocine
salt-and-pepper, but s*till there's no mobile, no clue* as we're powering
through the gloom and zig-zagging lights of new realities and
something's choked back, could be laughter or magic.

IV.

Our packed flesh sways, an orange line snakes over black pipes.
Breath not inhaled leaves mild tinges of garlic. Bulge says to
bulge *this fine line between us, it's an unbroken sheet of glass.*
Unseen infection can't infect when there's no option.

V.

The bus's polyphonic hums and rattles, drones of traffic, are
patterns of silence under that *zip* on someone's travel bag: a sound
intimate as rooms burst-into, loud and clear as lone undressing.

Wanted

You would like to 'like' those who take pains
to lurk, even here in darkness,
those blurred by isolation,
the inexplicably grim.

To others, you say please.
You're sorry.
Not even with that hat on.
But you do like their lupins.
You wouldn't mind the cats and dogs.

The ancients who grieve in your body
seemed to thrive in a dearth of men,
making do, and mending
oddballs, but sheer choice corrupts the vision

(flesh en masse becomes pale
mountains melting slowly
towards the end,
marked by interior disturbance,
disruptions from the hidden

wounds) … exposes habitual dreams'
purposeful imprecision.

And given this sensory deprivation,
you home in on the bare
bones, like irregular shaped holes
and bolted-on shards
in darkening shades looking for soulmates
to clink with.

All you can see is the stain
of outsider that you share with some,
must not share further,
as each of you looks to the other
to be saved

from an altered nature.
Yet in this deaf and mutes' competition
someone else is creeping out,
like you are carving a person,
filing away air they're not.

Shoppers in Mayfair

They've stepped
from white interiors into their heartland,
the heart of the matter, wearing
fine smokes. Seeing through mirrors.

Even the beige and velvety minors
sport that gloss for ease
of slippage. Success.
Galleries like these.

A sated quiet or bluish kiss-curls age them.

Low on the agenda, skies look remote.

Behind this block
a basement window's lime-lit
and one tattooed arm snips
round a paper jacket-pattern
marked like a body for theatre.

The Hidden Flaw

On an islet Henri makes
between his admirers
and the cliff's sheer drop

paints are lined up, old rags smeared
then folded neatly
onto stiffened towers.

They dry up pauses
in the rendering of surfaces,
random discharge
of taboos.

It's not about metaphor.
Or 'breaking through
under the radar'.

Colours and brushes are well looked after,
never argue back,
are partners in defining

how made-up dreams have no
design: fail to release him.

He doesn't see it yet,
lights another cigarette,
pours another shot of Calva.

Tate Modern Pigeon

Sirens, helicopters, voices
and the foils of rustled birches.
Against a busker's harp, the river.

On a red bench the fat son and father eat baguettes.
Not looking down, they kick out.

They sense only vermin, a shadow
advancing on happiness.

Not that wild tic,
delicate emergency.

Early Days – Half-Dreaming Your Bike Route Home

Between this moment and
BOOM!

night's hot stone, winking.
White-lit muscle and faces
flesh out red-light traffic.

I whisper, your lips zip…

River and parakeets
backflash at Hasidic Jews
or squeaked ice cracks, sinks,
the bus bowls through reflections,

alarms trip, eyes avert –
silhouettes, moored or grounded,
loom black in stilled reeds.

Skeleton vessels to homes
stake out a loamed darkness.

Your bicycle unreels
lone long-distance runners.

I almost…*I whisper, your lips*
zip, taught me shut it.
Love it.

(Boom)

For a Better World

For the Euston tunnellers

Capsules of human hurtle or smash a way through meta-worlds
(harmonies of the subtler networkers ungrasped before they burn).
Sleepless hearts, you tick under streets. Spines of snow crisp under lights;
the fluttering lost shadow tree stumps as tomorrow
tightens its grip on now. The dark-deprived robin sings.
How will we blossom for our children
and beyond: abandon these desires, and in time?

Oxford Users and their Dogs

The city is pretty with hope and skittering
shadow; behind its glass live ghosts are restless.

I'm watching your watchers' eyebrows arch
but what with your shouts and barking
drowning out strains

(silences they'll never hear), I guess you'll crash-on
not fearless but regardless

...try to believe buried selves
never give up the quest to haul us home.

Construction

You are on about X.
You worry about others
whose namelessness makes top of the list
when the rains have this biblical greed
to drown us.

Today with desk creaking
and all around it quiet, it is him:
his hand can't co-ordinate

between plate and piece of cake,
his shoes house too-long toenails
that make him bunch
toes down a twisting

staircase without proper rails –
and part of him dug foundations
for the self-shadowing

NOOO! that rose up, like some broch,
towered over – what? – shame?
Perhaps some rage
that had to be locked-up?

Was it, at first, supplication?

He's polite to everyone. Self-effacing.

You worry about the unnamed
always.

As if this might help
them name things.

Veils Failing

I.

A chill-fall of wisteria leaves
drowns the place in yellow silence

despite house sparrows shrieking.
The electric birch

weeps. New laws are chaos.
They strip Autumn of rose tints.

Where to look now.

Inwards.

II.

Infills are half-flooded fields foiled by skies
emptied by us,

deliver this pewter lining:
water's quiver of life, lifted

where a driftage of wintering gulls
answers a rumble of M40 cars.

But water faking

                  unaltered calm.

III.

Lose yourself, in vistas hazed
by vehicles or where windows'

blurred brittle glass
reveals nothing but chromed leaves,

that twig's *col legno* repeated.
Repeating.

Behind grazing green sheep
and an orange semblance
where bleached fields turn

reminders, or
a blackbird's song cuts

in millions of tiny plunges:
umbra.

Something in the Air, March 2020

Foaming spring: it bursts
with the waves of wild leaders.

The ache might be unappeased love,
more easily named, unharmed,

through distance.
Here it can live, safer untested. Still,

you're more real than anything
leading us on, including spring.

*

Each footstep feels ground I am numb to
and the rook's deep-throated *kraa*
abrades lacier birdsong;

the field is a floated
irregular shape settled in dips.

I'm unsettled mid titbits of information,
fake news. Panic stations.

Somewhere beyond screening
blackthorn and whitebeam,
further back,

things are kicking off. For now,
the ground imprints on my sole
its swollen dearness.

UK, Autumn 2020

'The Tories' biggest trick? Convincing the world
they have a cunning plan.'
— Marina Hyde

In the middle of the hill, a field.
In the middle of the field a little bush.
A blob of shadow clings to it.

The swell is nut brown,
yields only that 'navel', stones, a silence
you can see for miles. There are limitless
pile-ups of cloud above it,
swallows leaving.

A Perfect Storm, Christmas Eve

dear Father Christmas,
dear God – gods – please

night's busy stringing
the house with rain, irregular
thumps

(we're on our knees
choked by plastic

illuminations)

fusing climate, politics,

loves,

(give us a zillion splinters
of light, interfere

with us)

those at unthinkable risk. Edges
of sleep are reliable
(till we're forced to register
each suffering locked

out)

as cliffs to drop off,
then as you pedal through air,

the heart: it's shocked
back into night.

Heights of dark pull us down,
the world is calling

through fits of rain,

its patterns of pain
as yet unlearnt.

V.

Elective Surgery

I.

A weird ecliptic light.
Though birds are singing against
the battle and rip
of earth-moving equipment
everything is muffled.

II.

A sleepy woodpecker drills
intermittent holes in my dreams.
Waking has you walking in
to a private hospital.

*

Almost asleep, he drills.
It's weak, absent-minded,
like a tired habit of thinking.

There is something new
in the raw air. The blue is a dare
to love more, without arms,
lips, eyes, words, or even
enough understanding

(that is never completed).
The smashed skin of earth
will be smothered
but we have further work here.

I relearn, for the last time,
how you were never mine,
will never change.
The bird flies away,

the blade
slips beneath your skin.

Lacuna

Silver water trembles through blackness:
an owl's call arcs over
fridge-hum. The unflappable Joker
is lemon tree shadow
(lemon breath softens walls).

The path is a-glitter with flint.
An owl's call wobbles
on through sunlight. Cows inch
towards unimagined
night.

Answers:
not yet yours.

Only silvery scratches
owl chicks make on thought
return, as they message home.

Communication

As if it had been cruel gazing
with a blind useless eye
    the sky reaches down
touches the green cone of holly

dims it with orange
In its glut of cadmium spots
reactive to whatever Above
does the tree reflects
a wound leaked softened

    blurs
As if all obstacles
might now be dissolved
and only the holly
stood in a winter evening's calm

Mind in the Garden

Still. Unbending. The garden's verdure-patterned 'rooms'
stalk inattention, turn mind
to that granular darkness ants built into compost
fiddling minerals through a tickled deconstruction;
and there is no end.

Mind sets off at evening, as, crouched under lightening,
flattened bushes dim to
heighten noctules' pendula, tuned-up whites (*Syringa*)
banish in-between-things.
Night kills the blues.

Incy Wincy Spider

For Ayla

Gravel is thrown towards the past,
snail shells...
Nameless air answers.

'More', she says, 'more', and my hand
climbs her dress up ladders of rhyme.

My hand is an acorn's cup. Scoop
the fruit of her skull into its emptiness.

Remember, trust gets broken.
I post two blackberries
into a mouth that will tell,
lustful for those eyes, mapping.
Popping.

Breakdown

You stab at birdsong with disavowals,
muffled as a doped-up dreamer.

Bonelessly writing himself on blue,
a crow seems to spell it out
in the guiltless act of flying.

I offer a flint 'Cycladic head'
found in a quiet swollen by yews.

It passes through unsteady hands like water.

*

The slope is thick with spokes and frozen
arms. Silence is a gravitational force

holding the chalk in place,
allowing in one bird whose

single note, tremulous,
stretches through unexplored spaces,

searches like a parched tongue.
The answer's almost inaudible,

but it comes.

Muntjac

Himalayan balsam and quaking grasses
where woods dip, slip
into soaring meadow below a cloudless sky...
Nothing adds up.
You are old, the world has learnt so little,
you've not yet begun.
Are their words believable?

Risible?
This loner in a hurry
skims over man-made confusion,
stinks that mean us,
like flat stone to ocean.
She skips through this noon
commuter-belt woodland, leaves us
the silent.

With wind in her fur and fear's directives
she'll zigzag further
into a whole self's yearning,
bark it
into the evening air.

Two Poets

'A sentimentalist is simply one who wants to have the luxury of an emotion without paying for it.'
— Oscar Wilde

I. Poet at a Poetry Reading

Imagine the crawl of words
on skin that won't flinch.

Little's on show
but upright stillness:
an animal on the qui vive
for what feeds him.

His voice has negative spaces
where all that was discarded
lived.

Between the words
you hear its shapes
(and no ego:
mastered shyness).

What survives there simmers-
on in the lights of emptied stages.

II. Agape

Unprotected
under semantics'
clattering

his engender that thought
'lines not
impure',

steady an I
that shakes
from past trespasses –

give the other licence
to risk it.

You won't know its rarity
till it's there.

Untitled

I never met him, except through words

the shock has a dark side
flickers on thanks then
absences

the world that is him has no time for time
welcomes me when I recall
his premise that flaws are alive

we have no story to tell
alone each is fiction
the whole untellable

let the poem
unravel its own

Ghazal for Us All

Is it God or emptiness sending us survivors
a searchlight's breach of split cloud? A doubt might make us survivors.

We crawled, scratched, hid, fled, lied, half-died – were silenced.
Didn't realise. We were born breathless, plus survivors.

The journey is coiled up, long innards
invisible in the likes of us survivors.

Don't grip so hard on love, nor kick it into long grass:
you'll give us away (oh sleepless survivors).

New life waits inside the shells of sufferers,
shells (or perfect cases) made by us survivors.

The green-gold of June sucks at my edges.
I'm over-tender, precarious. That susurrus is us: survivors.

Nothing Changes

At last a field appears to shock us
(is it an end's sudden demands?),
it's haze above waist-height grass, flecks of bees,
gold-glazed after the river's

swans, mosaic of moneyed brightness,
even the towpath, dwindled to
'nothing':
a buzz of suggestion

when time has run out, time that arrests,
as we lightly retrace our steps –
as a beginning easily ends, is left there.

Notes

The Carpenter's Daughter's Long Engagement

Perbenismo (It.): respectability

Colours of Paris, 1984

Muguet (Fr.): lily of the valley.

Oeuf en gelée (Fr.): a speciality of French delicatessens consisting of a soft-boiled egg in aspic.

Vitrier (Fr.): a man who sold sheets of replacement glass, calling out the word as he trundled his barrow through the streets. Deep piles of lilac branches all around a particular church were part of a Catholic ritual that I witnessed.

The Tree Surgeon

Composite pose was a convention in Near Eastern and Egyptian art where a figure was represented with feet, legs, hips and head turned to the side but the torso facing the viewer. This is also known as *twisted perspective*.

Hints from Colour

Ronronnements (Fr.): purrs

(Avoir) le cafard (Fr.): depression; literally 'to have the cockroach,' from *Les Fleurs du Mal,* Baudelaire

Punctuation

Comma : any of several nymphalid butterflies (genus *Polygonia*) with a silver comma shape on the underside of the hind wings.

Comma: via Latin from Greek *komma* 'piece cut off, short clause', from *koptein* 'cut.'

Deep Winter

The quote from Giuseppe Ungaretti means 'I have never been so attached to life.' It is the final stanza of 'Veglia,' a short poem limning a night spent beside a dead fellow-soldier in WW1.

First Steps from Rupture

The phases listed in the poem are necessary for wounded skin to heal.

Veils Failing

Col legno (battuto)(It.): a musical directive to strike the string with the stick of the bow, literally 'with the wood.'

Two Poets

Agape (Ancient Greek: *agapē*) is a Greco-Christian term. It refers to a universal, unconditional, altruistic love that persists and transcends all obstacles through an effort of will. In its Christian form it stems from the mutual love between God and man, and was considered the highest of the Greek forms of love.

Two Rivers Press has been publishing in and about Reading
since 1994. Founded by the artist Peter Hay (1951–2003),
the press continues to delight readers, local and further afield,
with its varied list of individually designed,
thought-provoking books.